It Started at 2, Not 2:15

THE IMPORTANCE OF BEING ON TIME AND NOT LATE

BY

STEWART MARSHALL GULLEY

2017

Contents

Myself   1

Starting Off   5

Traffic   7

Work   11

Date?   15

School   19

Church   21

Funerals   23

Weddings   25

Meetings   27

Theatre, Concerts &c.   29

Appointments   31

Bills   33

Travel   37

Friends   39

Transportation   41

Cars   43

RSVP   45

My 11 Year Old's Birthday Party   47

Service People   49

The Worst Thing You Could Ever Do   51

Parable of the 10 Virgins   55

My Agreement to Time   59

Biography   61

Myself

With all of the titles listed in this book I have been a victim of each, being late at one point or the other. However, it is not a known reputation of mine of being late. If anything they would be saying, "He's going to do it and he'll be here on time."

There are people, without a doubt, regardless of the situation or the event, who are late, and many feel nothing of it unless they are penalized. Even then they may have an argument to justify why they are late. And then there are some who pay the late fee and think nothing of it, because money is no problem and they feel nothing that everyone has to wait for them.

My mother was a very timely person. If you told her 3 o'clock, rest assured she'd be looking out the window for you at 3.

I was in the service industry for at least 25 years as a stylist and barber. I was used to appointments and know some of the problems that arise when someone arrives late and you still took them, or when something went wrong in the shampoo bowl, un-expectedly. Unplanned events can cause you to get behind for the next appointment. Customers do tend to tell little fibs about their hair stating there's no chemicals in them, and when you proceed to perform a particular service you find out there *is* and there's a reaction with the hair product used. What a bummer! The next client is on time and it puts you 45 minutes behind to immediately correct the problem. Not only that, if you have 10 clients scheduled for the day and the first one is late and you still take them, it is going to throw the whole day off. Some operators refuse to do them and they have to reschedule or charge a late fee and then they have to be worked into the schedule when convenient. It's similar to a doctor performing routine surgery that usually takes only 2 hours; if he ends up running into difficulties, he could be there performing an eight hour surgery. We're not talking about situations like that in this case. We're talking about a person who, for some unknown reason, doesn't value their time, or yours, and is constantly late. If there's the small possibility of an excuse for being late, they will find it. The bottom line is that they started off late and, as the poet said, "time waits for no man". They never fully figured out preparation time and traffic. And to this person that is driving, to them everyone is driving too slow, can't drive or is simply in the way.

The unrealized thought is that if your appointment is at 2 o'clock and you walk in the door at 2, you are late. You should have signed in already and have been seated waiting to be called. Can you imagine walking in at 2 and there's a line of about 15 people in front of you? This will cause you to get to the window at 2:15, 2:30 or even later. And you have the gall to be upset. Your appointment was at 2 and not 2:15.

I had a friend named Willie who was to start a new job. His scheduled time was to be there at 8:00 am. For some unseen reason he arrives on his first day at 8:30 am. Unfortunately, there was no mercy and he was fired before he started. The boss told him that he hired him for 8:00 am and not 8:30. End of story! In other words, we're not going to start off this way. Remember, if you don't get to work a little earlier than you're supposed to you are late. They are not paying you to *get ready* to start, they are paying you to *start*.

I also had a co-worker at a salon I first worked at when I got out of school. I was an assistant and did all of the dirty work. After a while I was able to build my own clientèle and I became very skillful. However, a young lady had worked there for years and had a very large clientéle. She was constantly late every day and over a period of time her clientéle became slow. I recalled one day that I was doing clients and she wasn't, but she was waiting at the salon hoping someone would come in. My, how things can change all because of time and your attitude about it.

Starting Off

Let's get first things first. Whether you wake up by alarm, self, service company or a friend calls you, there must be ample time to prepare regardless of where you are going. You have dressed yourself for years and you have a pretty good idea of how long it takes. But for some unknown reason many people refuse to prepare the night before, or weeks ahead if it is something formal. It is something about that last minute adrenaline that gets a person moving quickly and not taking a lot of time thinking of what to wear. Everything is a rush, from taking the shower, to a quick breakfast and running out the front door. However there's an old saying that haste makes waste. And sometimes, being very quick you run into a problem and then all of that time is wasted because you didn't take your time. What if it's your favorite dress or trousers and you're in a hurry and you ripped off the zipper? Now that's a blast! Now you're mad at the clothes and everything in the room that's in your way, all the way to the loaded closet of clothes that you have to search through to find something else to wear; and, God forbid, should it need ironing. Now you're really set behind.

For those who prepare ahead, it is always smooth sailing even when something unexpected does occur. Try it, you just may like it. The less stress we create, the better off we are. Most of us will run into enough problems of other peoples' making, so there's no need to create some for ourselves unnecessarily. We will meet a lot of people throughout the day who are in a rush, causing problems and accidents. This brings me to our next subject... *traffic*.

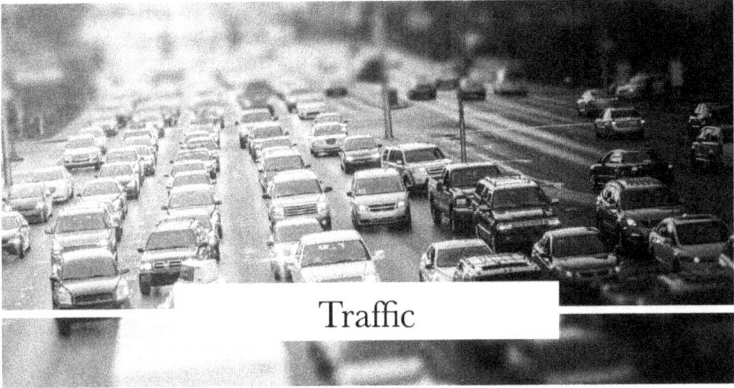

Traffic

Ticket, road rage, towing, frustration

Do you know how much traffic you can run into by leaving 10 to 15 minutes late? Some people stay at work an extra hour so they won't be sitting in a traffic jam. However, everyone can't get on the freeway at the same time, even if they left work a little earlier, but it will help if allowed.

Whether going to work, theater or any appointment, if you don't allow for traffic and parking you have already screwed up your day. The aggravation of fighting traffic and to find a parking space is enough to drive you to an insane asylum.

There are a lot of people in the world today with cars. For instance, if a husband and wife has four children of driving age, each one of them may have a car along with the husband and wife, and all are on the same road during certain hours.

Not only are you fighting the road rage traffic, but also the little lady who takes her car out once a week – and she's *never* in a hurry. Now you're huffing and puffing and saying she should have stayed home. Well she did stay home until it was time for her to go out, and she planned it. You should understand that many elderly have to drive because their family, friends and organizations don't have time for them. They have paved their way in society, and when they get old they are being dumped. My mother drove until she was about 80.

Not only will you go through that, but allowing for parking could drive you just as crazy, even if there is a parking lot. What if it's one of those spiral parking lots and you have to be careful traveling up and most of the lower levels are full so you have to go to the top and you were due to be at work, or your appointment, ten minutes ago. By the time you park you are totally frustrated and you fly out the car, run down the steps, and you trip and fall and sprain your ankle. Oh, what a day! How much is this day going to cost you? You paid for parking, you can't work and now there's the doctor bill. Whew!

Better yet, you were in such a hurry that you didn't realize you parked in the handicapped parking. Prior to falling, you were not handicapped and you return to your car to see a juicy $250 ticket on the windshield. Are you getting the picture? God forbid if you parked wrongly in a place where they tow away vehicles. If they towed your car, it'll be about $450; someone will be rubbing their hands and be very happy that you were in a hurry and not paying attention. Parking signs are so tricky. It seems as though they are crafted in such a way that no one can understand them, so you can get a ticket from money running out the short term meter or no parking hours.

I can't remember exactly where the situation was that I'm about to mention, but there was an event and there were a lot of cars parked on one side of a nearby sign that clearly stated: *No Parking.*

However, everyone came up and saw a car parked there and they figured it must have been ok. But to their surprise the city made a lot of money towing cars that day. Unless there's a parking attendant, or police, out there saying it's ok, I wouldn't trust it.

A couple of years before my mother passed away she wanted to give me her car. It was a clean-running economy car. I was always busy and didn't own a car at that time. I told her I didn't want it because I didn't have a parking garage and I didn't want to worry about moving the car from one side of street to the other. Let alone think of all the cars on the street already, insurance, gas, and repairs. People thought I was crazy because I didn't want it. To me some gifts people can keep. Lol. I didn't own a car for about 25 years and had opened several businesses and had a couple of houses without one. I knew what I wanted to do and when I wanted to do it, and very seldom did someone pick me up for anything. I told them I will be there, because I knew the bus schedule and sometimes people with cars will make you late, because they wait until the last minute to do anything. These days, we thank God for companies like *Uber* and *Lyft*. Normally one of their cars is within 5 minutes or so when you need it.

For those who take the bus, you must also allow for problems, although buses do run pretty close to their schedules. Ironically, I was a half an hour late the other day, and I left on time. However, the bus company gave me the wrong corner! When I got there I called them again and the next scheduler gave me the correct time and corner. Also, it doesn't happen often, but buses do break down, forcing riders to offload and wait for the next one.

When using the bus, you also have to allow time to walk to your destination after getting off. Walking is good, but allow time for it. Years ago, before there were lots of cars on the roads, people walked and had plenty of energy and stayed slender. Now a lot of health problems and much fatigue.

Penalty: Ticket, accident, frustration

Work

We are living in a time where lots of people are out of work. Many of these out-of-work people would make great employees. However you may jeopardize your job by being constantly late or undependable. Even if you're the owner. Peoples' attitudes are that they can be late to your business, but you can't. If the doors said they open at 8:00am, rest assured there'll be someone who has been standing there since 7:45 or earlier. Your lateness can change the personality of anyone and you may think nothing of it. Bosses may smile at you, but sometimes in the back of their mind they are trying to figure out how to fire you, or you fire yourself. Lateness is a serious business.

One day, I was telling a person about people who were late to work every day and the supervisor allowed it. Not the boss, he knew nothing of it. The supervisor gave you favor and everyone noticed it and the workers began to bicker among themselves. Over a period of time, for some reason the supervisor was fired and moved on, and a new supervisor was appointed. The new supervisor was no joke. The first time someone came in thirty minutes late the supervisor docked their pay. You noticed it on your check and you were angry as heck. All of the other employees heard the commotion, but they were happy that someone finally stood up to you. You personally were very angry and wanted to call the supervisor all sorts of names, but they were only doing their job. It was the former supervisor who went along with you, only to make you worse. As far as the new supervisor was concerned you didn't work that half an hour so you shouldn't get paid for it. The funny part about it was that you were the boss's nephew. Lol

Whatever the reason your job does not pay you to wash your hands, fold up your jacket, or get a cup of coffee before you start work. Although this happens, it is not proper unless your job calls for it. All preparation should be done before you punch the clock, unless you are punching in a few minutes early and it's not overtime.

People have no idea how much difference a few minutes can make if you are on the other side of the door. It shows respect and concern when you're on time. We know that things can happen, but for the most part you're late because you want to be and will have a hissy fit if someone says something about it. Not only that, this person will have a bad customer attitude all day. I had a niece who worked for me. She had a bad attitude and reading this book I'm sure you have a good idea of what I did. Yes, you got it, I fired her.

Rest assured someone will be waiting for your position, but it has to be handled legally or there will be a lawsuit. If the contract says 8:00 am and you're there 8:15, who broke the contract? Either stay hired or get fired!

Never try to give a reason for confrontation or getting fired because of being late. You may have to relieve someone at a certain time and you being late they have to wait until you get there which may cause them to be late somewhere else. What if this person has a child that has to be picked up from the nursery and is charged because they are late? They were closing at 6 and all the children are gone except theirs. Are you going to pay it for them? Better yet, because they left 20 minutes late they run into extra traffic which causes them to be an hour late. Can you see the domino effect?

One time, I recall having one particular customer who was always late and usually she was my last one. So I had to wait until she got there. I got fed up and when she was 20 minutes or more late I would leave and was not concerned about the money I lost. Enough was enough.

Penalty: Loss of job, no promotion, no raise, looking to smoothly be replaced

Don't think you are not being watched! They are looking for the right opportunity to fire you. Sometimes you are punished for being late and other times mercy has been given to you. However, sometimes mercy runs out!

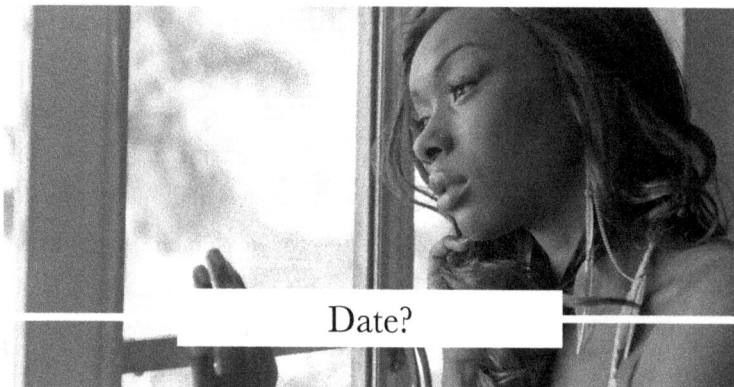

Date?

It's a late dinner date at your girlfriend's house. She expects you to be there at 7:30pm. All that day, all she talked about with her friends was that you were coming over that night and it was going to be a special night and there will be sparks. She ordered beautiful lingerie for that evening and she went to the market to pick up steak, potatoes, salad and your favorite wine. She took the time to marinate the steak and also picked up some beautiful candles. She pulled out her favorite linen because she was going full charge. Of course the bedroom was all freshened with the finest sheets and scented candles. You called her around 4pm to see how her day was going and she sounded so happy and cheerful on the phone that you were coming. After a half an hour conversation she hung up and began to prepare the salad and other things needed for the dinner. Of course the aroma of the freshly baked pie was gently filtering throughout the house. By now it's around 6:00pm and she runs to take a bubble bath, perfumes up, and slips into the sexiest red dress you had ever seen. It is now about 7:15 and you're expected at 7:30. She really doesn't like eating this late, but it was going to be a special dinner. She places the steaks on the grill and they begin to sizzle, and to finish them off she thought she'd put them in the oven for 10 minutes. It is now 7:40, but there is no sign of you. Her anticipation is still high, although it was a slight let down because you're ten minutes late, so far. She has to take the steaks out of the oven and she begins to pace the floor continually looking at her watch; it's 8:15 and her joy bubble has been busted. She thought she'd call you to see what was going on, but for some reason you didn't answer the phone and now she decides to make another phone call to her best friend and she's in a rage. It is 8:45 and now she has had it. Unfortunately, he stopped by a buddy's house and got into a deep conversation about a sports game and didn't realize what time it was until one of his buddy's said, "Man, I thought you had a dinner date." "Oh, shoot," he said and takes off running to his car. He picks up the phone to call her and there's no answer and he doesn't know what to do. He finally gets to her house and knocks on the door and there's no answer. He looks in the garage and doesn't see her car. What do you think going to happen?

Moral: When things are important you stay focused, because you may have only one chance to make it right and it's the first one.

Think about it. How much money and time it took to prepare all that she did. Money + time + wrong conversation = disappointment for both.

This can also work in reverse, when he's going to pick her up. He's on time, but she lives by that old fable, "You need to make him wait a little while." He gets there and you are still pampering; the whole dinner becomes a disaster simply because you were not on time. He may have bought tickets to a show as well and you both will be late for that. He's not trying to be angry, but in his

16

heart he's saying a lot of things that I don't think you'd like to hear.

Penalty: May lose a relationship, respect, he/she may feel his friends are more important.

School

It is important to get an education these days, but being late to get it is very frustrating, especially if you're driving. Not only are you rushing, mad at drivers, but you miss out on the introduction of each class daily. You feel nothing about asking the person next to you what was the lesson or discussion about. In reality the person is trying to be nice and to answer your questions, but their real feeling is that you're late every day and you're not paying them to get your lesson or take notes for you. They don't want to miss a special point by taking the time to explain to you what the instructor said earlier.

Somewhere the late issue has to yield a great penalty. Otherwise there's no lesson learned. We all are late sometimes due to uncontrollable circumstances. But when you're late every day there's not too much concern, because you're getting away with it. A friend of mine noticed I had set a clock 15 minutes fast. He said that, to him, it didn't make sense because every time I looked at the clock I had to take 15 minutes off.

The teacher is in the middle of an important lesson and you come rushing through with coat, books and bag, looking for a seat. Everyone wishes you had never come to class at all. Others are serious about the class. You're only there because you might be getting paid to go or are being forced to go to school. However, if you're suspended then you're mad at the instructor and the school and want to bad mouth them.

When I was a teenager I was late to school 2 or 3 times a week. The sad thing about it was that we lived only two blocks from the school. During the earlier years, before becoming a teenager, we would get a swat from the principal for being late. Oh my God, you would not hear of anything like that today. Today, they don't have to show up to school at all and you better not touch them.

Just to give you an idea of how I thought as a kid. When I was in kindergarten if we were late the teacher would give us a slip to take home to our parents to sign. Well, one day I was late and I took the slip home, but my mother never saw it because I signed it myself and took it back to school the next day, and the teacher accepted it. I loved art so I was able to copy my mother's handwriting at 5 years old.

Even though, these days, many students are taking online classes you still have to discipline yourself. Just because you're at home you still can be late on doing the lesson. Late is always late.

Penalty: Loss of education, missing important introduction of lesson, no one wants to be bothered with you to give you information.

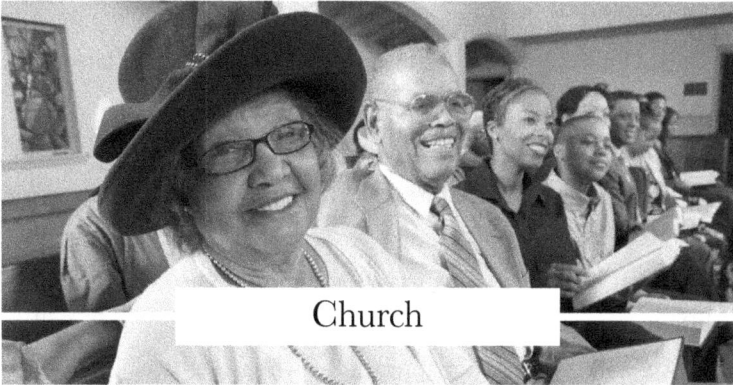

Church

Church is just like any other business. They run on a schedule. Many times people are late only because they started out late, due to watching something on TV, or being on the phone. Some are late so they can make a grand entrance so everyone can see what they have on. The pastor is in the middle of a great message and here you come strolling in wanting people to slide down or you pass over them to find a seat.

When I was about 11 years old my stepfather gave me a few swats for not leaving for Sunday School on time. The ironic thing was that when I got there his deacons were not there to open the church and a few of us were standing outside waiting to get in because *they* were late. To me, my stepfather should have been there and given the deacons a few swats, when they finally arrived!

The best cure for latecomers to church that I've seen is to fill the church from the front. When the front was full they then filled up the remaining rows. Therefore if you came in late there was no place for you to sit but in the back because everything up front was full. Of course you will have some of those from old school saying, "That's Sister Robert's seat and you can't sit there because she has been sitting there for years." So in other words if she's late the seat is vacant and everyone has to wait to see if she's coming late or not at all. Did she call and say she was not coming?

When you walk in a service late those in the pulpit will be looking straight at you and your entrance can cause a person to lose a thought. But what do you care, as far as you are concerned they should not have been paying you attention. Who could miss you with all the designer clothes you had on and that arrogant walk.

Trust me, you are not appreciated when you come into places and people have to make room for you, especially when you could have been on time. This is very upsetting to men who make an effort to come to church on time, and women come in late expecting men to give up their seat for them. Some men would say that you should have been on time and watch you squirm for a seat. Or in your mind you would say, "Where are the gentlemen who would not let a lady have a seat?" Personally a *real* lady would have been there on time.

Penalty: In the view of others causing disturbance. Missing something you should have heard. Being secretly talked about. Causes others to miss something that was said, which also could have been beneficial to you.

Funerals

Will the deceased ever be respected? Some funerals have been held up because a certain person wasn't there yet. Some people feel nothing. Either they want to show people how much they were mourning when they brought them in or it's strictly for show. You knew about the funeral all week so why couldn't you be on time. If they were paying you like your job you would have been there on time.

When funerals are held up it can put a damper on the whole service. All eyes are on you when you're late and trying to find a seat and God forbid you're the type that creates a scene because there's no seat for you up front. You are not the popular one that day, the deceased is. The rule is "Early to the front and late to the back."

I just attended a nice funeral and as the praise dancers were dancing, here comes about 5 people coming to the front trying to find a seat and blocking the view of the dancers. I may be wrong for this, but it tickles me when latecomers come to the front and can't find a seat. What do you expect? Sometimes we have to take the initiative ourselves and fill in the seats, otherwise someone may come with a large hat and block everyone's view. God forbid they are a talker. Trust me I've seen them come in and chatter away in conversation during a funeral.

Many problems are already caused at a funeral, whether it's from how the deceased looked, program, parking or anything a person can think of and then you're late with an attitude because there's no seat. Keep living, you will have your time to be the star in the casket, but respect those who have preceded you.

This may sound strange, however, they take offerings for everything else in church. I feel they should take an offering for a funeral as well without all of the conversation pushing people to give. It's just a little something extra for the family. The funny part of this would be who would be the person that would receive it?

Penalty: May cause the whole funeral to be delayed, damper on the whole funeral, and you may look like a person who doesn't respect the deceased and just there for show.

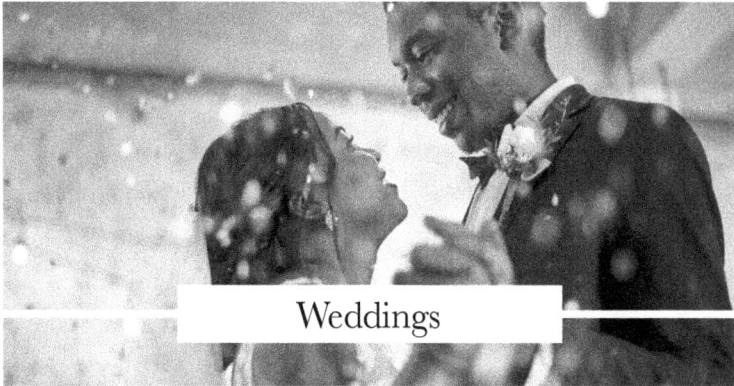

Weddings

This is another area of life where a lot of problems can occur, just like funerals. We all know that things can accidentally happen, but if you fail to plan and use the proper professional people, you should expect anything to happen and it could turn out like improvisation comedy.

Starting a wedding late will set the whole pace for the ceremony. It will cause people to be on edge wondering when it's going to start. Attendees have made sacrifices by taking the day off work, as well as spending money for a new outfit and purchasing a gift.

You had planned for this day 6 months ago so what happened that you were not paying attention. Did you have different responsible people in charge and not trying to do it all yourself? A wedding to me is like a play or a stage production. Everyone has has to play their part on time and on cue otherwise it will throw others off.

I had a customer one time sitting in my chair and she asked me did I know anything about weddings. I said, "I have a great idea about them, so what's the problem." My background was mostly in theatre writing and directing plays, so to me it was just another production. It was four days before the actual wedding and they hadn't had a rehearsal or knew how to put anything together. The best they had done already was knowing who was bringing food, and the gowns and tuxedos were absolutely beautiful. So, I asked her when was their rehearsal going to be, and I told her that I'd be there to help. It was magic to me. I found out what songs they wanted and I conducted the whole wedding rehearsal. Now the new surprise was that they didn't have any type of program. Lol. So, I used my computer and designed and printed a program as well. One more thing, I guess I was a Godsend to them because the photographer had no idea of what types of pictures to take, so I conducted that as well.

The point is that everything does not work out that way and when you're late on any task it's like a domino effect and causes a problem in every area.

Penalty: Putting a whole damper on the wedding. Upsetting the wedding party. Even though people say they understand they really don't unless you had a heart attack or in an accident. Usher will not allow you to come in because the wedding has started. If it was important enough you should have been there an hour earlier even though you had to sit and hoping they started on time.

Meetings

There are thousands of meetings taking place every day and unfortunately someone is always late. You are the star of the show that day if you are late, and it is not for favorable reasons. There is not a lot to say on this subject, but late is late. Whatever your reason may be, sometimes it's not good enough; like others, deal with it and move on. You may have a positive message for them, but if you're late you really have to wait about 10 to 15 minutes for them to warm up to you, because they felt you have wasted their time. Hopefully you had something that they really wanted. Even if a flight was delayed, or a train was canceled, the bottom line is that you were not there at the scheduled time. We know that unfortunate things happen, but let's try not to let it be our fault. One time I was late for a meeting and came to realize I missed the whole meeting when I got there, because I had the wrong day.

Try to be at meetings before or on time. Someone has to get there first. Believe it or not, people in meetings often want to hurry up and get it over with. Talking business for a long time can be stressful. Basically, the leader wants to express *when we do it, how we do it, where we do it* and *will we make any money by doing it*? Most people have adapted the feeling of the microwave oven. Everyone is in a hurry, so much of a hurry that we can tell the microwave to hurry up.

Penalty: Looked at as a non-responsible person regardless of the reason you were late. People upset that they may have to explain to you over what they talked about. Or all disgusted waiting for you if you were the one that called the meeting and was late.

Theatre, Concerts &c.

Plays, theatre etc. You should at least arrive half an hour before it starts, and an hour wouldn't hurt. And I don't mean just driving up in the parking lot at that time, but present in the theatre. However, producers should be mindful that you've already been there a half hour or so and expect them to start on time. People are even irritable if a play is suppose to start at 7 and it starts at 7:15. They start looking at their watches or cell phones. The frustrating thing about reserved seating with tickets is that if you're late you're still guaranteed a seat in your designated spot. Therefore whatever time you come in you have to cross over people and it is very rude and disturbing. Something they wanted to see in a split second you stood in front of them and thought nothing of it because you paid for your ticket. Some theatres will not allow you to be seated until intermission.

Some people never realize that you have to get to events early. If an auditorium holds 1000 seats and the show starts at 8. Wouldn't it be chaos if 1000 people got to the front door at 7:55 trying to get in and get to their seats, all wondering if the show is going to start on time at 8.

Penalty: People upset that you are walking in front of them while the movie/play has started, especially if there was something special they wanted to hear that helped the plot. You can really make them upset if you spilled popcorn or soda while passing by. You may have spoiled their evening. Being late puts a lot of mental pressure on you.

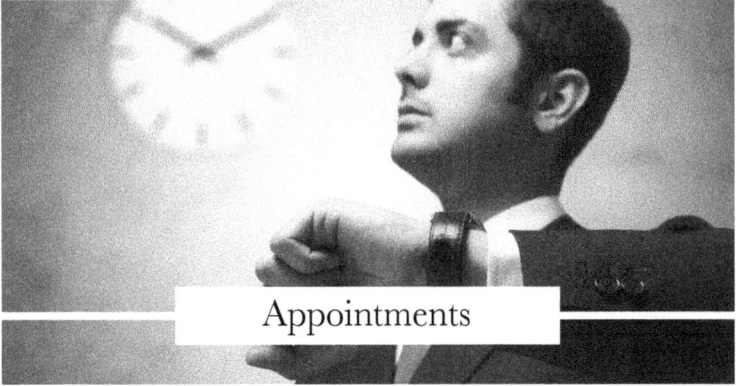

Appointments

Remember this is a very large world you live in and you are not alone. Therefore appointments are important. Even if they can't take you right away at least you're in the door. Sometimes, some professionals have to stay and work overtime to accommodate you because certain things didn't go right during the day. They still respect your time if you're willing to wait and they will work overtime. If you think the world is chaotic with appointments think how crazy it would be without them.

Penalty: May have to be rebooked and you have driven a long way. May have to wait and extra hour or two if they still take you. May cause a person a little irritation that you were late and they still accept you. When you are late for certain appointments you may not get all the services that you need or even suggested, because the service provider is trying to get ready for the next appointment that is on time.

Bills

Companies have made lots and lots of money from people being late with their telephone bills, electric bills, not to mention Pay Day loans. Despite what you may think, credit card companies love it when you're late. They charge you a small fee for a telephone bill being late. You may say they will charge you $4.00 for being late. All they need is 1000 people to do that a month and they will get a free $4000. Yes pennies add up. The thing about being late on these bills is that you may have the money, but refuse to pay on time. They don't mind you being late, but it will show up on your next bill in small print. Sometimes you don't even know you're paying a late fee because you just pay it and as long as the fees are close to what you've been paying you don't pay it much attention. Boy, would I love to get $4000 a month for nothing. Late mortgage and rent fees all add up.

Think about it, say for instance that you didn't want a particular service because it was $5.00 more than another service you were comparing it with. For example, one service was $35 while the other same type of service was $30. You chose the $30 because it was cheaper. However you are always late on your payments and they charge $35. Now, you are still paying the $35.

Penalty: Extra late fees, services cut off which will cause an inconvenience. Now you have to pay late fees and go stand in line. Possible late fees shown on credit report or have to go through a lot of prompts to pay bill on phone.

WARNING

Beware of all late fees

A. Lot of late fees are in very fine print. If you do not see them be sure to ask

B. Mark the day on a calendar of anything that is a 7 day trial. Try to cancel on the 6th day.

C. Also some may give a 14 day trial, but the trial starts on the day you ordered and not the day you received it. So if it's 2 days getting there you have only 12 days.

D. Some companies will give you a 30 trial before they charge. However, if you want to cancel before the 30 days are up some will still want to charge you for the product. You must understand these are marketers and it's all about the money.

E. Some companies will send you a trial fee, but you must pay the $4.95 shipping charge. A lot of times that is in very small print or shows up after they get all your information.

Also in extra small print is the actual price of product if you do not cancel on time. This price can range from $50 to $100. And if you call a day after they will tell you that it is shipped out, whether it is shipped out or not. Also be careful about the automatic renewal in small print which will be charging your credit card if you do not cancel.

Remember to write the phone number to cancel immediately when it's shown. Sometimes it's hard to find after you order product. There's an order number and a cancellation number sometimes.

F. Moving violation/ parking ticket fees all should be paid on time. If not the late fees can cost you hundreds of dollars in late fees especially if the ticket turns into a warrant. If I get a ticket I usually try to keep it in my wallet for a while if I paid it. I don't necessarily trust the digital world and if the police stop me and calls in and they said it doesn't show I paid for a ticket who do you think they will believe? But I have my proof!

G. Believe it or not I once got a ticket for eating peanuts on the train ramp in Los Angeles. Where I was sitting on the ramp you couldn't see the *no eating* sign, plus when you found it you noticed it was very small. I had only a couple of peanuts in my mouth and the patrol came up to me and showed me their badge and said I was on camera for eating peanuts. I went to court and the fine was $160. Because I didn't have that much money on me I had to go home and pay it on the computer and they charged me an extra $10, so now it's $170. The legal system will always be right regardless of what you say. So, if I had gotten mad at court they could have thrown me in jail and also fined me, which would be more money for them. Or if I chose not to pay the ticket by the time the extension day was due it could have turned into a warrant and possibly cost me $500. Still more money for them.

I recall cancelling a membership at the YMCA and because I didn't give them a 15 day notice they charged me for the full month. After you go to the gym for a while who can remember about the 15 day notice unless it's posted?

Everyone wants to make a little extra money in this world if they can figure out how to charge you!

Travel

Trains, buses, planes, ships, and any other type of transportation all have schedules and people book their times around them. That's why many times they ask you to be there 1 to 2 hours ahead in case of security or parking problems. If your flight leaves at 9:00 am you are definitely late and will miss it if you pull up in the parking lot at 8:55 am. How in the world will you be able to check in baggage, go through security and go almost a mile to get to the plane. On top of that, what if you're in a wheelchair?

Penalty: May miss flight or any other type of transportation such as train or bus. Have to wait several hours for the next one. In some cases have to wait the next day. May cause change of plans of everyone that was waiting for you a certain hour on the other end. Big inconvenience of everyone.

Friends

This is one area that many people disrespect that can cause a whole evening to become a disappointing one. Some people feel that just because they are your friend they have a right to be late and cause you to wait for them. It turns the whole evening sour because of your disrespectful attitude. Some friends do not invite you to events because it is embarrassing knowing how late you often are. What could be worse if you're late and have a loud, rude mouth. Not only do people see you, but hear you and will be thinking the worst of you.

Usually, I can figure out how a person may be at their job by seeing only how they treat me. Meaning, if they are late all the time for me they are late for work too. If they are not late they almost kill a person on the road trying to get there. Their job is important, but friendship is something they have on the side so they think.

Disrespecting your friend's time can cause a lot of problems.

If you treat everyone like they were the President of the United States, a Pastor, City Official, or someone of high rank, or even God himself when it comes to time, you will do fine. Because certain people have a certain rank in life others tend to respect their time and be there at the appointed time. Some feel they can be a little late and it's ok. It's like smoking a cigarette. Start a little habit and it can become greater and many don't like cigarette smokers around them.

I recall a friend inviting me to a play and we arrived late. He dropped me off in front of the theatre, and he rushed off to find a parking spot. It was a small theatre, however, and the manager held up the play so that my friend could get a parking space because they were closing the door and didn't want any interruptions. The main reason why is because how the theatre was made you could see people coming in late. Instead of coming in the back you had to come through the front and the audience could see you. I just held my head down, but we all survived.

Penalty: Loss of friendship, friends feel you don't respect their time. Not being invited to special events, because you will make them look bad for arriving late.

Transportation

Regardless of whether you're on time or late, I have never understood why people know what it costs to get on the plane, bus or any other transportation yet they wait until the last minute to start looking for their money, which will cause a delay. I've seen so many people who will stand and wait for the bus 30 minutes and when it comes they get on and start looking for their money or card. Didn't they know or see the bus coming? It can be very annoying. They can turn a Rapid Bus or Express Bus into a regular bus because the driver is waiting for you to find your money. When you finally put the money in it gets stuck, so the driver is behind schedule trying to push money down. Many just tell you to go ahead and have a seat and they will work with the coin box when they get a chance. God forbid he should see you running to catch the bus and he decides to wait and when you get on you have to start looking for your money which is way down in the corner of your purse.

Penalty: You will get doors shut in your face as they are pulling off. Many times they cannot make an abrupt stop for you, because it can cause an accident for those standing, which can also cause a suit for the bus company especially for those who are looking for a suit in anything.

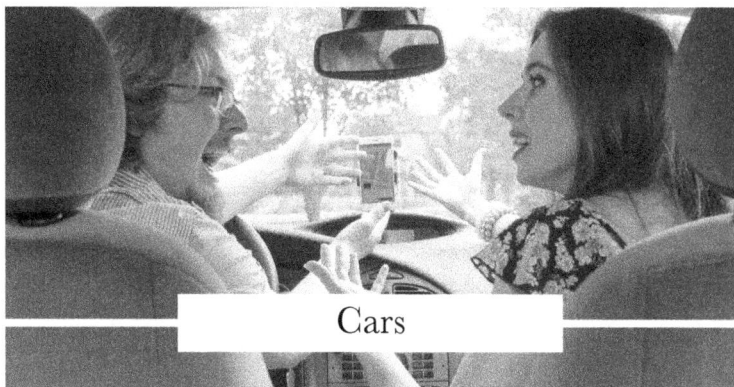

Cars

I understand that there are some jobs you definitely need your car and there are some just for convenience. But people with cars take chances on rushing at the last minute and all of a sudden their fussing all the way because people aren't moving fast enough as mentioned earlier. The ironic thing I've found that some people who have cars can make you late if they were to pick you up. To yourself you would be saying: I could have caught the bus and been on time! But their attitude is that you're ungrateful especially if you get upset.

Can you imagine a friend or spouse being home all day and you get off at 5pm, but you have to stand outside a whole extra half an hour because they were late. If it wasn't an accident it would be hard to understand. Now you both have an attitude riding home. When that clock say you're off, you're ready to go home.

Penalty: A very angry person that is grateful, but not ungrateful as many would think. Why spoil the day?

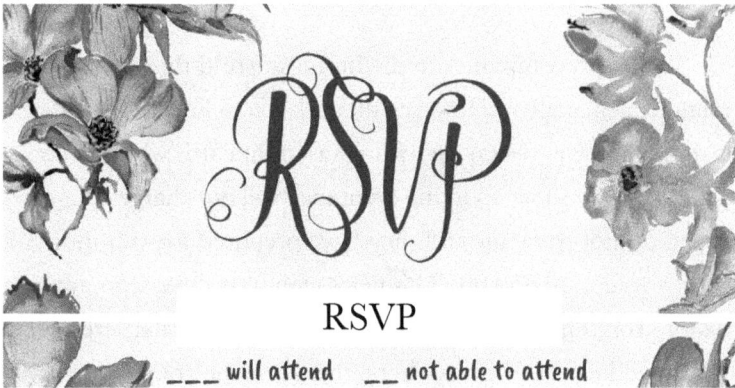

RSVP

___ will attend   __ not able to attend

The term RSVP comes from the French expression *"répondez s'il vous plaît"*, meaning *"please respond"*. If this is written on an invitation it means the host would like to know if you are going to attend the event. Another kind gesture in this is the fact that they thought enough of you to think that you'd respond to let them know whether or not you are able to attend. If you do not RSVP, you may face a few consequences, such as waiting in another line until those who did respond are present. If special gifts are being passed out, it is not fair for you to be there on time and did not RSVP and receive a gift. Therefore those who did RSVP are shortened. By you responding it also helps to let them know that you received the invitation in the mail or email. Another thought would be if the host has someone else call all those who were on the list to see if they received the invitation. A good follow-up program.

If you do not RSVP and the host was preparing food for 20 and 40 show up, it can also cause a problem. It is common courtesy to respond. As stated, they thought enough of you to spend their money and prepare for the event. At least you can respond. People have been known to cancel an event if enough people do not respond.

There are companies in the business world that hold special events which are free. However, they ask you to RSVP. The process is that you have to sign up with your credit card, which is about $50.00. If you show up to the event they will not charge your card. If you do not show up and they have prepared for you they will charge your card $50.00. This helps eliminate those who just sign up for everything, but do not show up, only because it's free.

So, to help hosts everywhere, the next time you get an invitation...

JUST be a great responder!
JUST don't forget to respond if the invitation requests you to
JUST pick up the phone
JUST email you're coming or not
JUST mail the RSVP card
JUST DO IT!

And hosts everywhere will thank you and every person who learns how to be a perfect responder for making this aspect of party hosting a breeze!

From announcingit.com

Penalty: Loss of respect

My 11 Year Old's Birthday Party

This segment very much relates to the subject you just read. When I was 11 years old I had my first real birthday party. My mother had prepared the food, drinks, and ordered the cake as well. All of the children were told and given an invitation for that day. However it must have rained cats and dogs. Strangely enough not one soul came nor did anyone call and said they could not make it because of the rain or any other reason. Any type of RSVP would have been appreciated. It was a slightly depressing day, however, for some reason I overlooked what had happened and my two sisters and I had the party amongst ourselves. I said more cake and ice cream for me. I'm sure I would have felt much better if at least someone had called. All the years had gone by and I had never given myself a birthday party. I had refused to. I did end up having 3 small parties and they were all surprises. Those were the only parties I had in my life. Now in my 60's I don't wait for anyone to celebrate my birthday and people that know me know that I love birthday cake. My birthday is in November, but I eat birthday cake all year around. It can be January and if I feel like getting a birthday cake with my name on it I do so. Or I just may buy a small piece from the Supermarket. Why wait! I have often wondered what kind of party would I give myself. I'm sure it would be a full production, due to the artist and playwright within me.

Service People

Unfortunately, people who render a service are not exempt from being late. If a certain deadline is due, a person should try their best to meet it. I've seen lateness in many things, from Funeral Programs to Wedding Programs. Contractors, printers and gardeners all can be late. What can happen sometimes is that some of these services take on more jobs than they can handle. Or they may start your job and a bigger job comes along, that pays more and it causes them to put your job on the back burner.

Let's think about it this way. Say, for instance, that you contacted a printing company to do a job for you and it was due on February 12. You had taken everything in on February the 1st, which was ample time. Although you only had to pay $200 for your job, they didn't know you had plenty of additional work that would have come to $3,000. This is what happened: the printer happened to take a rush job from an unknown company. He was going to make $1,000 from it. He took the job a few days before your deadline which threw everything off for you. What he also didn't know was that was a one-time job, because they usually use another company and a problem arose, but they were going back to use them when everything was corrected. You made your original customer upset because their work was late and they decided to go with someone else after they've received the work. Therefore the printer was losing 2 customers, plus lost an additional $3,000 of work, just to please a customer that was going to pay $1000 for a one-time job. Referral business is the best thing in the world. You will not have to sell the client that calls you if their friend referred them to you. They just about already had told them everything about you from your promptness to how you look.

As we know there are some things that happen to service people that are beyond their control which may put them behind. Hopefully it's a good reason and doesn't cause you to lose clients. Good news travels just as fast as bad news.

Penalty: Will lose customers.

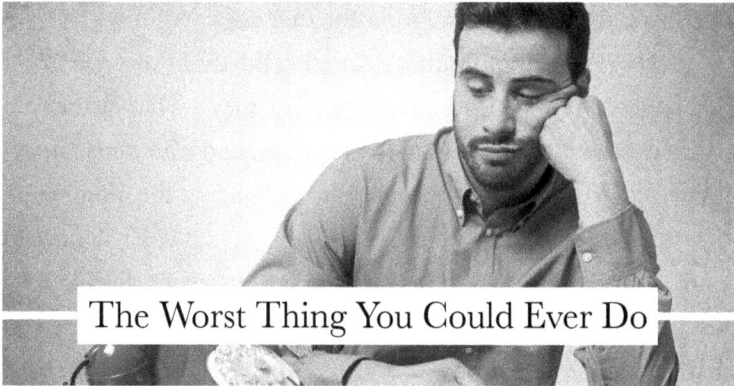

The Worst Thing You Could Ever Do

This little paragraph does not take a lot of explaining, but the worst thing you can ever do is not call and say you are not coming. I could never understand how a person could do this and when they see you they feel that you should understand, because that's just how you are. It's bad enough being late, but not to call at all has a lot of stigma to it. Basically it's saying that the person is not that important. Can you imagine preparing a dinner for someone and they never showed up or called and said they were not coming. Better yet a doctor's or hairstylist appointment and you don't say anything. This is why some services fine you for broken appointments because you didn't call in advance and say you were not coming. Someone else could have taken that spot. Who wants to lose money or time?

What is also amazing is, for example, when you have an appointment at 11:00, but you call at 11:00 and say that you can't make it. You knew you weren't coming at 10. Why didn't you call then? People respect you more if you call way in advance, because someone may want to take that appointment.

Respect a person's time and they will respect yours. And if they don't, you'd had better find someone that does!

Being late is not grand, it's disrespectful and everyone is not that happy to see you like you thought! Yes, they are happy that you made it so that the presentation can go on and everyone can get home. When you are late, people have to build up the momentum of happiness all over again to appreciate you and you will have to work harder at it for them to gain your respect again. People have lost great jobs and deals because they were late. The only person that we say is never late is God and even then we feel He could have done things earlier and on time according to us and our problem.

As a reminder everything is not cut throat. There are times when things happen that are not foreseen, which can be a surgery that takes longer, accident, hairstylist problem with hair, sprained your ankle or lots of reasons that things can happen. But if none of those occurred, you just didn't respect their time nor your own, because you've made them upset for being late and your nerves were very bad trying to rush and get there, wondering how would they receive you if you were late.

Being late is like having a car accident on the freeway. Everyone has to wait until it's cleared to proceed. In other words everyone has to wait for you to arrive to start!

Want to see how much people respect your event, dinner or job you've given them? Watch what time they get there.

I recalled having a grand opening for a salon and it was from 2:00 pm until 6:00 pm. Amazing some were there during the duration and some came very late which was almost 6:00. They all laughed at me because I turned the music off at 6:00 and thanked them all for coming!. One person said, "Well the invitation did say from 2 to 6." I knew I had to clean up the mess and they all were going home and I wasn't expecting any volunteers to help, so I did what I knew so I could get home at a decent time as well.

Some people are so hardcore on people not calling that if they got a phone call stating that you had died, they wish you had called a day before to let them know so business may continue as usual. lol

Penalty: Never being invited again or not allowed to make appointments.

Parable of the 10 Virgins: The importance of preparing and being on time

[1] "At that time the kingdom of heaven will be like ten virgins who took their lamps and went out to meet the bridegroom. [2]Five of them were foolish and five were wise. [3]The foolish ones took their lamps but did not take any oil with them. [4]The wise ones, however, took oil in jars along with their lamps. [5]The bridegroom was a long time in coming, and they all became drowsy and fell asleep.

[6]"At midnight the cry rang out: 'Here's the bridegroom! Come out to meet him!' [7]"Then all the virgins woke up and trimmed their lamps. [8]The foolish ones said to the wise, 'Give us some of your oil; our lamps are going out.'

[9]"'No,' they replied, 'there may not be enough for both us and you. Instead, go to those who sell oil and buy some for yourselves.'

[10]"But while they were on their way to buy the oil, the bridegroom arrived. The virgins who were ready went in with him to the wedding banquet. And the door was shut.

[11]"Later the others also came. 'Lord, Lord,' they said, 'open the door for us!' [12]"But he replied, 'Truly I tell you, I don't know

you.' ¹³"Therefore keep watch, because you do not know the day or the hour.

$$-\text{Matthew 25: 1-13}$$

Penalty: Not preparing and being late may cause you to lose the enjoyment of a wonderful event that you will never forget.

WARNING!

Keep being late and you may lose job, friendship, car, house, health, respect, money and so on.

Is being late all the time worth it?

·

My Agreement to Time

I, _____, will try to do my best to be on time everywhere I go. I do realize that people have taken their time to prepare for me and I should respect all of their hard efforts. I also will do my best to be at work on time or anywhere that I am paid, because they believed in me and they expect me to deliver for what they hired me for. Although I have friends I will try my best to respect their time as well because there's nothing like a good friend you can depend on. Whatever I am attending regardless of the venue I will try to be there at least an half an hour to an hour in advance, because I realize there are many people attending and the event would love to start on time. Someone has to be first attending. I also will not take myself through a lot of stress at the last minute by not preparing or disrespecting myself. I do realize accidents will happen in life, but I will try my best not to allow the accident be caused by me, which will cause me to be late and cause others to be on edge waiting for my arrival. I will try to do my best in all areas, because I do understand there are consequences at being late.

Sincerely,

_____

Signature   Date

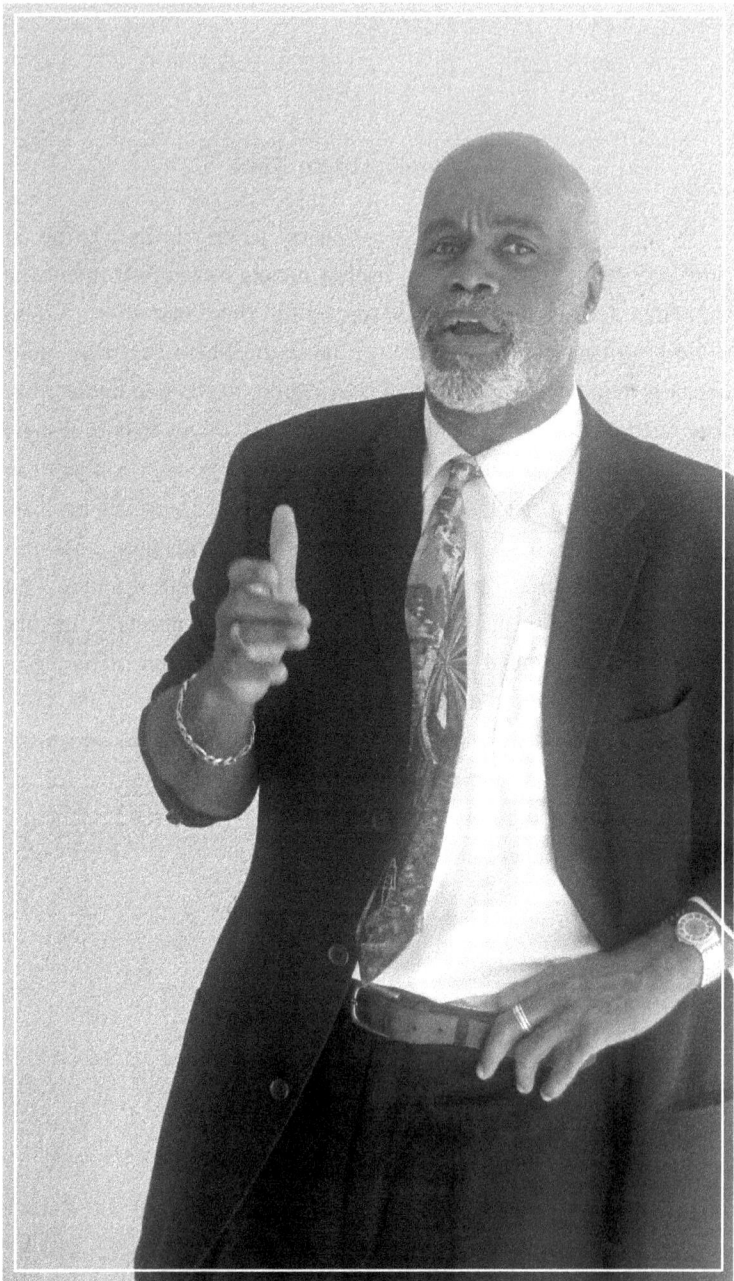

Biography

STEWART MARSHALL GULLEY, best selling author has often been called The Renaissance Man because of his many professional talents. A producer, playwright, author, real estate agent, cosmetology instructor, and an inspirational speaker are only a partial list of his phenomenal gifts and accomplishments. Many see him as a very comical person and most agree he should have been a stand-up comedian; however his more serious side manages to come through his self-help and fiction books.

Find out more about Stewart at:

www.stewartmarshallgulley.com

Other Books

Novels:
Love Should Have Brought You Home Last Night
High Heels and Bad Feet
Eric, the Last Child

Inspirational Self Help:
Buck Naked (Stripping yourself and becoming who you really are)
Who in The Hell Is They
Stay in Your Own Lane
How to Get Over a Past Relationship

Children's Book
His Eye is On the Sparrow (Which includes Coloring Book and
Comprehensive Test)
The Birthday Party to Which Nobody Came
The Elephant and the Mouse

More to come...

www.ingramcontent.com/pod-product-compliance
Lightning Source LLC
Chambersburg PA
CBHW070826210326
41520CB00011B/2134